Contents

T0367047

Introduction

1   The purpose of this Historic England Good Practice Advice note is to provide information to assist local authorities, planning and other consultants, owners, applicants and other interested parties in implementing historic environment policy in the National Planning Policy Framework (NPPF) and the related guidance given in the National Planning Practice Guide (PPG). This good practice advice acknowledges the primacy of relevant legislation and the NPPF and PPG. While it supports the implementation of national policy it does not constitute a statement of Government policy itself, nor does it seek to prescribe a single methodology or particular data sources. Alternative approaches may be equally acceptable, provided they are demonstrably compliant with legislation, national policies and objectives.

2   The advice in this document, in accordance with the NPPF, emphasises that all information requirements and assessment work in support of plan-making and heritage protection needs to be proportionate to the significance of the heritage assets affected and the impact on the significance of those heritage assets. At the same time, those taking decisions need sufficient information to understand the issues and formulate balanced policies (NPPF Paragraphs 157-8, 169-70 and 192).

NPPF requirements

3   The NPPF sets out in various different places a number of requirements for Local Plans in respect of the historic environment. Local Plans need to:

1   be based on adequate, up-to-date and relevant evidence about the economic, social and environmental characteristics and prospects of the area – which would include the historic environment. In particular this up-to-date evidence should be used to assess the significance of heritage assets and the contribution they make to the environment (NPPF Paragraphs 158 and 169)

2   set out a positive and clear strategy for the conservation, enjoyment and enhancement of the historic environment (NPPF, Paragraphs 126 and 157)

3   contain strategic policies to deliver the conservation and enhancement of the historic environment (NPPF, Paragraph 156), and

4   identify land where development would be inappropriate because of its (environmental or) historic significance (NPPF, Paragraph 157)

Gathering evidence

4   When gathering evidence, it is important to bear in mind that this is not simply an exercise in setting out known sites but, rather, in understanding the value to society (ie the significance) of sites both known (such as those on the National Heritage List for England, see www.HistoricEngland.org.uk/listing/the-list) and potential, without which an understanding of the sometimes subtle qualities of the local distinctiveness and character of the local area may be easily lost. In particular:

■   In some cases, it might be necessary to identify heritage assets outside a local authority area, eg where there are likely to be setting impacts caused by potential development proposals within that area

■   Some asset types are not currently well-recorded. *The Register of Parks and Gardens of Historic Interest in England*, for example, is thought to represent only around two-thirds of sites potentially deserving inclusion

■   Evidence gathering can help identify parts of a locality that may be worthy of designation as a Conservation Area, or may merit local listing

■   Assessing the likelihood of currently unidentified heritage assets being discovered, particularly sites of historic and/or archaeological interest, will help to future proof the plan

5   It may be helpful to collate this information within a Heritage Topic Paper to draw together the evidence prepared and the subsequent implications and actions required.

Sources of evidence

6   Sources of evidence to assist in gathering information include:

■   the National Heritage List for England: www.HistoricEngland.org.uk/listing/the-list

■   the Heritage Gateway: www.heritagegateway.org.uk/gateway/

■   Historic Environment Record (HER): local planning authorities should either maintain or have access to a Historic Environment Record (NPPF, Paragraph 169) – see Heritage Gateway to find your local HER

■   Conservation Area Appraisals and Management Plans – see relevant pages of the local authority website(s)

■   Local Lists – as above

■   National and local 'Heritage at Risk' registers: www.HistoricEngland.org.uk/advice/heritage-at-risk

■   Historic characterisation assessments – see Heritage Gateway to find your local HER

■   World Heritage Site Management Plans – see relevant pages of the local authority website(s)

■   In-house and local knowledge and other expertise (ie civic societies, local history groups, neighbourhood consultations, the Civic Voice: www.civicvoice.org.uk/)

7   Where the evidence base for the historic environment is weak, local planning authorities may need to commission proportionate research, for example:

■ detailed historic characterisation work assessing the impact of a proposal for a major urban extension or rural development

■ visual impact assessments, considering the potential impact of allocations upon the setting of important heritage assets

■ seeking the views of the local community about what they value about the historic environment of their local area (NPPF, Paragraph 155)

■ an appropriate archaeological assessment to consider whether heritage assets with archaeological potential are likely to be present in areas where the HER indicates that there has been little or no previous investigation

8   Work in putting together Local Plans will often generate new evidence of the state and significance of the historic environment. Documents, such as historic landscape characterisations, strategic environmental assessments, conservation area appraisals, economic development studies and those supporting supplementary planning documents and local listing assessments, will often contain new evidence. Local planning authorities will find it useful to collect this information and make it publicly available, including through the Historic Environment Record. The information can be invaluable in improving plan-making and decision-making in the future and is of significant public benefit in furthering the understanding of our surroundings and our past.

Application of evidence

9   The evidence base for the historic environment may also assist with the preparation of the following:

■ assessments developed to meet the goal of achieving economic, social and environmental gains jointly and simultaneously, ie through land availability, etc (NPPF, Paragraph 8)

■ the Sustainability Appraisal which accompanies the Local Plan, **and**

■ appropriate indicators for monitoring the delivery of the plan

A positive strategy for conservation and enjoyment of the historic environment

10   A positive strategy in the terms of NPPF paragraphs 9 and 126 is not a passive exercise but requires a plan for the maintenance and use of heritage assets and for the delivery of development including within their setting that will afford appropriate protection for the asset(s) and make a positive contribution to local character and distinctiveness.

11   This strategic approach can inform all aspects of the planning system by recognising and reinforcing the historic significance of places. As part of a sound conservation strategy, policies for local housing, retail and transport, for example, may need to be tailored to achieve the positive improvements in the historic environment that the NPPF expects (NPPF, Paragraph 8). Conservation is certainly not a stand-alone exercise satisfied by stand-alone policies that repeat the NPPF objectives.

12   Consequently, the Local Plan might need to consider the inter-relationship of the objectives for the historic environment with the following:

- **Building a strong, competitive economy**
  – How might the plan conserve and enhance the quality of the historic environment in order to encourage tourism, help create successful places for businesses to locate and attract inward investment? What opportunities are there for heritage-led regeneration?

- **Ensuring the vitality of town centres**
  – What role can the historic environment play in increasing the vitality and attractiveness of town and village centres?

- **Supporting a prosperous rural economy**
  – What opportunities does the reuse or adaptation of traditional buildings provide for supporting the rural economy or providing homes for local people? What potential is there for new heritage-led tourism initiatives?

- **Promoting sustainable transport**
  – How might new roads and other transport infrastructure be delivered in a manner which also conserves the historic environment of the area? Could the introduction of sustainable transport initiatives offer related opportunities for heritage through improving street/ traffic management or public realm enhancement at the same time?

- **Delivering a wide choice of high quality homes**
  – How might the plan encourage adaptive reuse of historic buildings? How might new residential developments best be integrated into historic areas?

- **Requiring good design**
  – How might the defining characteristics of each part of the plan area be reinforced in the approach to design?

- **Protecting Green Belt land**
  – How might the policies for the Green Belt and the definition of its boundaries be tailored to protect the special character and setting of a historic town?

- **Meeting the challenge of climate change, flooding and coastal change**
  – How might flood prevention measures be provided which also safeguard the heritage assets in the area? How might the strategy for renewable energy developments and associated infrastructure reduce the potential harm to the historic environment?

- **Conserving and enhancing the natural environment**
  – How might the plan best identify, protect and enhance important historic landscapes? What contribution might the strategy for improving the Green Infrastructure network also make to the enhancement of the area's heritage assets?

- **Facilitating the sustainable use of minerals (see box)**
  – How might any impacts of mineral development on an area's heritage assets be controlled to acceptable levels? How might the plan safeguard potential sources of building and roofing stone, or improve archaeological knowledge through approved mineral operations?

> Further advice is available in *Mineral Extraction and Archaeology: A Practice Guide,* English Heritage on behalf of the Minerals Historic Environment Forum, 2008. As this predates the NPPF, the document is currently under revision.

13   In formulating the strategy it is advisable and often necessary to consider the following factors:

- How the historic environment can assist the delivery of the positive strategy and the economic, social and environmental objectives for the plan area (NPPF, Paragraphs 126 and 132 and Sections 66 and 72 of the Planning (Listed Buildings & Conservation Areas) Act 1990)

- How the plan will address particular issues identified during the development of the evidence base, including heritage at risk and the reuse of buildings

- The location, design and use of future development and how it can contribute to local identity and distinctiveness

- The interrelationship between conservation of heritage assets and green infrastructure, landscape, regeneration, economic development, transport works, infrastructure planning, tourism, social and cultural assets, town centres and climate change mitigation/adaptation (NPPF, Paragraph 126)

- The means by which new development in and around World Heritage Sites and other designated heritage assets might enhance or better reveal their Outstanding Universal Value and significance (NPPF, Paragraph 137)

- The means by which new development in Conservation Areas and within the setting of heritage assets might enhance or better reveal their significance (NPPF, Paragraph 137)

- How Article 4 Directions may be employed to provide an additional conservation mechanism

- How HERs and local lists might assist in identifying and managing the conservation of non-designated heritage assets

- How the archaeology of the plan area might be managed

- The possible role for CIL and/or s106 in delivery of required infrastructure

- Whether master plans or design briefs need to be prepared for significant sites where major change is proposed

- What implementation partners need to be identified in order to deliver the positive strategy

- What indicators should be used to monitor the heritage strategy's effectiveness

- In order to deliver an effective strategy for the conservation of the historic environment, is there a need for the plan to include Development Management Policies and where appropriate specific policies for specific assets or specific areas within the plan area?

Strategic policies for the conservation of the historic environment

14   The plan will be the starting point for decisions on planning applications and neighbourhood plans are only required to be in general conformity with the strategic policies of the Local Plan (NPPF, Paragraph 184). Consequently, sustainably managing the historic environment is best achieved by identifying clear strategic policies for heritage, in order to assist those preparing neighbourhood plans.

Identifying inappropriate development

15   The local plan needs to assess whether or not it should identify any areas where certain types of development might need to be limited or would be inappropriate due to the impact that they might have upon the historic environment (NPPF, Paragraph 157). This might include, for example, tall buildings within identified view corridors.

Development Management Policies for the historic environment

16   Specific Development Management Policies may be needed in order for decision-takers to determine how they should react to an application affecting a heritage asset. Such circumstances could include the following:

■   **Those areas where Development Management Policies are necessary to amplify a general, overarching, Strategic Policy for the historic environment within a Core Strategy of the Local Plan** – for instance, to deal with particularly distinctive or important historic environment features or significance

■   **Those areas where further clarity would be useful** – for instance, how local planning authorities determine applications affecting archaeological remains of less than national importance

■   **Those areas where Development Management Policies may be necessary to address the local circumstances of the Plan area** - for example, to clarify the approach to development within an Area of Archaeological Importance (see box), or to protect or enhance important views and vistas

■   **Those circumstances where Development Management Policies are needed to address particular cross-boundary issues** – such as World Heritage Sites, National Parks and Areas of Outstanding Natural Beauty whose management is carried out by joint working between several local planning authorities or the management of those extensive historic landscapes which run across a number of authority areas

> Sections 33-35, Ancient Monuments and Archaeological Areas Act, 1979. For further information see www.HistoricEngland.org.uk/advice/hpg/has/archaeologicalimportance/ although it should be noted that only five such areas have ever been designated.

Site allocations

17   A conservation strategy can help with site allocations in terms of considering environmental and policy constraints against the evidence in the relevant Strategic Housing Market Assessment (Planning Minister's letter to Chief Planners 19 December 2014 www.gov.uk/government/publications/strategic-housing-market-assessments).

18   It can identify opportunities to conserve the historic environment, such as site allocations positively addressing heritage assets at risk, and can help to ensure that site allocations avoid harming the significance of heritage assets (including effects on their setting). The strategy can also be used to inform the nature of allocations so development responds to and reflects local character. Site allocations should be informed by an evidence base and an analysis of potential effects on heritage assets. Further advice will be available in the forthcoming Historic England Advice Note on heritage considerations for site allocations in local plans.

Planning across boundaries

19   Conservation of the historic environment may involve cross-boundary issues, where development proposals near the boundary of one local authority area potentially affect the setting of heritage assets in another. In such cases in exercising the Duty to Cooperate both authorities need to take into account the impact on the conservation and enhancement of the historic environment as one of the strategic priorities (NPPF, Paragraphs 156 and 178).

Cumulative impact

20   The cumulative impact of incremental small-scale changes may have as great an effect on the significance of a heritage asset as a larger scale development. Consequently LPAs may consider covering this issue in a specific Local Plan historic environment policy. In appropriate circumstances this policy could be delivered via an Article 4 Direction in a conservation area.

Nationally Significant Infrastructure Projects

21   There is a separate planning regime for Nationally Significant Infrastructure Projects (NSIPs) under the Planning Act 2008. See http://infrastructure.planningportal.gov.uk/ for further details.

Marine Planning

22   Some authorities have coastal boundaries and consideration will need to be given to marine heritage which may arise and the points above will equally apply. In England marine planning is administered by the Marine Management Organisation (MMO). For further details see: www.gov.uk/government/collections/marine-planning-in-england#about-marine-planning

Community Infrastructure Levy (CIL)

23   When preparing a CIL Charging Schedule, local authorities may wish to take account of any impacts of proposed levy rates on the economic viability of the re-use of heritage assets and heritage led regeneration projects.

Section 106 agreements

24   To support the delivery of the Plan's heritage strategy it may be considered appropriate to include reference to the role of Section 106 agreements in relation to heritage assets, particularly those at risk. Subject to meeting the policy tests in paragraph 204 of the NPPF, types of contribution might include:

- repair, restoration or maintenance of a heritage asset(s) and their setting

- increased public access and improved signage to and from heritage assets

- interpretation panels/historical information and public open days

- production and implementation of up-to-date Conservation Area management plans and appraisals

- measures for investigation, preservation and display of archaeological remains and sites

- provision of local capacity for the storage of, and public access to, archives resulting from archaeological and/or historical investigation

- dissemination of historic environment information for public/school education and research, including museum displays for popularisation of archaeological discoveries

- sustainability improvements (such as loft insulation) for historic buildings

- public realm obligations, including enhancement of historic squares and spaces, registered parks and gardens, historic pavement materials, street furniture, removal of street clutter and installation of sympathetic lighting, etc

Infrastructure Delivery Plans

25   Investment in infrastructure could assist in the delivery of the plan's strategy for the historic environment. For example:

- Open space, including wider public realm improvements for historic streets and squares

- Repairs and improvements to and the maintenance of heritage assets, including transport infrastructure such as historic bridges and stations, green and social infrastructure such as parks & gardens and sporting or recreational facilities

- 'In kind' payments, including land transfers

Supplementary Planning Documents (SPDs)

26   A heritage SPD brought forward in line with paragraph 153 of the NPPF can be a useful tool to amplify and elaborate on the delivery of the positive heritage strategy in the Local Plan and some local planning authorities may choose to support their conservation strategy within the Local Plan using a topic-specific SPD. There may be heritage considerations in other types of SPDs, for example flood management.

Strategic Environmental Assessments (SEA)/Sustainability Appraisals (SA)

27   In identifying the significant environmental effects that are likely to occur, an SEA/SA will recommend an appropriate response to the cconservation and enhancement of the historic environment. English Heritage published revised advice on preparing SEA/SAs in 2013.

Neighbourhood Plans

28   A full and proper understanding of the heritage of the local area is the most appropriate starting point for town and parish councils and neighbourhood forums to both propose boundaries of the neighbourhood plan area and develop policies that support and encourage the conservation and enhancement of the historic environment.

29   Including heritage matters in a neighbourhood plan will help ensure that new development is integrated with what is already exists and can demonstrate where standard design and construction may not be appropriate. This can encourage sensitive development of historic buildings and places that can invigorate an area.

30   Draft neighbourhood plans, neighbourhood development orders and community right to build orders have to meet certain general 'basic conditions' before they can be put to an independent examination (having regard to legislation, national policies and advice, being in general conformity with strategic local policies; contributing to the achievement of sustainable development an being compatible with EU obligations and Human Rights).

Neighbourhood development orders and community right to build orders must also meet additional conditions relating specifically to heritage assets through:

- having special regard to the desirability of preserving any listed building or its setting or any features of special architectural or historic interest that it possesses, **and**

- having special regard to the desirability of preserving or enhancing the character or appearance of any conservation area (Schedule 4B of the Town and Country Planning Act 1990 (Schedule 10 of the Localism Act)

31   Attention is also drawn to national policies and advice on the historic environment, such as that contained in the NPPF and the DCMS Statement on Scheduled Monuments & Nationally Important but Non-Scheduled Monuments.

32   Plans need to include enough information about local heritage to guide decisions, in particular, what it is about a local area that people value, and therefore, requires conservation and enhancement. That information will need to be based on robust evidence, such as the relevant HER. Historic England has published advice to assist local communities considering a neighbourhood plan.

Contact Historic England

East Midlands
2nd Floor, Windsor House
Cliftonville
Northampton NN1 5BE
Tel: 01604 735400
Email: eastmidlands@HistoricEngland.org.uk

East of England
Brooklands
24 Brooklands Avenue
Cambridge CB2 2BU
Tel: 01223 582700
Email: eastofengland@HistoricEngland.org.uk

Fort Cumberland
Fort Cumberland Road
Eastney
Portsmouth PO4 9LD
Tel: 023 9285 6704
Email: fort.cumberland@HistoricEngland.org.uk

London
1 Waterhouse Square
138-142 Holborn
London EC1N 2ST
Tel: 020 7973 3000
Email: london@HistoricEngland.org.uk

North East
Bessie Surtees House
41–44 Sandhill
Newcastle Upon Tyne
NE1 3JF
Tel: 0191 269 1200
Email: northeast@HistoricEngland.org.uk

North West
Suites 3.3 and 3.4
Canada House
3 Chepstow Street
Manchester M1 5FW
Tel: 0161 242 1400
Email: northwest@HistoricEngland.org.uk

South East
Eastgate Court
195-205 High Street
Guildford GU1 3EH
Tel: 01483 252000
Email: southeast@HistoricEngland.org.uk

South West
29 Queen Square
Bristol BS1 4ND
Tel: 0117 975 0700
Email: southwest@HistoricEngland.org.uk

Swindon
The Engine House
Fire Fly Avenue
Swindon SN2 2EH
Tel: 01793 414700
Email: swindon@HistoricEngland.org.uk

West Midlands
The Axis
10 Holliday Street
Birmingham B1 1TG
Tel: 0121 625 6820
Email: westmidlands@HistoricEngland.org.uk

Yorkshire
37 Tanner Row
York YO1 6WP
Tel: 01904 601901
Email: yorkshire@HistoricEngland.org.uk

Printed and bound by CPI Group (UK) Ltd, Croydon, CR0 4YY